MW00571363

Songs and Ballads

Essential Poets Series 53

Federico Garcia Lorca

Songs
and Ballads

In English Versions
by Robin Skelton

Guernica
Toronto/New York/Lancaster
1997

'Lament for Ignacio Sanchez Mejias'
appeared in *The Malahat Review*.

Antonio D'Alfonso, Editor
Guernica Editions Inc.
P.O. Box 117, Station P, Toronto (ON), Canada M5S 2S6
250 Sonwil Drive, Buffalo, New York 14225-5512 U.S.A.
Gazelle, Falcon House, Queen Square, Lancaster LA1 1RN UK

Second Printing.

Legal Deposit — First Quarter.
National Library of Canada.

Canada Cataloguing in Publication Data
Garcia Lorca, Federico, 1898-1936
Songs and Ballads
(Essential poets ; 53)
Translation from the Spanish.
ISBN 0-920717-65-9
I. Skelton, Robin, 1925- . II. Title. III. Series.
PQ6613.A763A28 1992 861'.62.62 C91-090309-3

Contents

II. 1924-1935

Preface

It is over fifty years since Federico Garcia Lorca was murdered on August 19th 1936, by the fascists of Granada. He was his country's most popular poet, and his death was immediately perceived as martyrdom. His reputation as a great modern European poet was established for English readers first of all by the publication of two small selections of his work: *Lament for the Death of a Bullfighter and Other Poems*, translated by A.L. Lloyd (1937), and *Poems by F. Garcia Lorca*, translated by J.L. Gili and Stephen Spender (1939) with an Introduction by R. Martinez Nadal. This was followed by a *Selected Poems* from the same hands in 1943, without Martinez Nadal's Introduction. In March and April 1942 a long essay by Arturo Barea was published in the magazine *Horizon*, and issued in 1944 as a book with the title *Lorca: The Poet and the People*. Edwin Honig's critical study, *Garcia Lorca,* was published the same year. Roy Campbell's *Lorca: An Appreciation of His Poetry* appeared in 1952. Other essays in English followed, and a number of book-length studies, as well as further translations of selections of the poems, most notably those by Rolfe Humphries (1953) and Philip Cummings (1976). Additional translations have been published by W.S. Merwin, Lysander Kemp, Norman di Giovanni, and Ben Belitt, among others. A *Selected Poems* in translation by many hands was published by *New Directions* in 1955.

Lorca's full use of the rich ambiguities of the Spanish language in which one word can often have many quite disparate meanings, together with his use of a symbolism that is often rooted in Andalusian folk-lore and sometimes in private obsessions, make his work peculiarly challenging to the translator. I have derived much help from the work of previous translators and commentators, but have gone my own way in attempting to echo, if not imitate, Lorca's extraordinary verbal music, and in using, from time to time, English words and phrases which appear to me to be equivalent to the Spanish, but which are certainly not correct in terms of literal translation. In the great *Lament for Ignacio Sanchez Mejias*, I have chosen to vary the thunderous refrain of the first section, in order to give the poem on the page a touch of the variety it would be given by alterations of tone, speed, and pitch, by a performer. Similarly in *The Martyrdom of Saint Eulalia*, I have chosen to repeat the name 'Eulalia' on several occasions for reasons of rhythm, and because, again, I see the poem as a 'performance poem'. Indeed all Lorca's poems are 'performance poems'. They were intended to be spoken, sung, chanted, and not merely read. It is this aspect of the poems that I have tried to emphasize in my versions.

Lorca was extremely slow to publish his poems in book form. His *Poema de canto Jondo*, for example, was published in 1931, ten years after it was written, and the *Canciones*, written in 1922, were not published until 1927. He clearly must have thought long and hard before giving his work the final assent for book publication. The poems I have chosen for this selection were all published in Lorca's lifetime. I am deeply grateful to George McWhirter for looking over my work and helping me solve many knotty problems. Whatever successes I have achieved owe a great deal to him; the infelicities are all my own.

Robin Skelton
Victoria, B.C.

I
1921-1924

Ballad of the Waters of the Sea

The sea
smiles from the distance
with teeth of foam,
lips of the sky.

'What are you selling, troubled girl
with the wind on your breasts?'

'Sir, I am selling the waters
of the seas.'

'What are you carrying, little dark boy,
mixed in with your blood?'

'Sir, I am carrying the waters
of the seas.'

'Where do these salty tears
come from, Mother?'

'Sir, I am weeping the waters
of the seas.'

'This bitter seriousness, heart,
where was it born?'

In the bitterness of the waters
of the seas.'

The sea smiles from the distance
with teeth of foam,
lips of the sky.

Balcony

Lola is singing
Songs to Our Lady.
The tiny bullfighters
are ringing her round,
and the barber is nodding
his wee little head
to the beat of the rhythm.
Between the sweet basil
and the green mint,
Lola is singing
Songs to Our Lady,
that very same Lola
who gazed for so long
on herself in the pool.

Variations

The air's unmoving water
under the echo's bough.

The water's unmoving water
under the stars' leaves.

Your mouth's unmoving water
under a thicket of kisses.

Half Moon

How peaceful is the sky!
The moon sweeps over the water,
scything, slowly, slowly
the ancient trembling river;
meanwhile a little frog
believes her to be his mirror.

Harlequin

The red breast of the sun.
The blue breast of the moon.

The torso half of coral,
half of silver and shadows.

Little Song of Seville

Daybreak
in the orange grove.
Golden bees
are garnering honey.

Where will the honey
be found?

In the blue flower,
Isobel,
in this flower
of rosemary.

A little gold chair
for the Moor.
A flashy chair
for his wife.

Daybreak
in the orange grove.

Snail

They have brought me a snail

within it a song,
an ocean of maps.
My heart
fills with water,
with tiny fish
of shadows and silver.

They have brought me a snail.

The Lizard is Sorrowing

The he-lizard wails,
the she-lizard is wailing,

the she and he lizard
in tiny white aprons

have lost unintentionally
their new wedding ring,

their little lead ring,
their small ring of lead.

Huge, unpeopled, the sky,
a balloon, lifts up birds.

The sun, a round captain,
wears a waistcoat of satin.

See how ancient they are,
how ancient these lizards.

Oh how they wail and wail,
how they keep wailing.

Silly Song

Mother,
I wish I were silver.

Son,
you would be so cold.

Mother,
I wish I were water.

Son,
you would be so cold.

Mother,
stitch me on your pillow.

Yes! That I will do
right now!

Song of the Rider (1860)

In the dark
of a highwayman's moon,
the spurs are singing

'Where, small sad horse,
are you taking your dead rider?'

the hard spurs
of the unmoving bandit
who dropped his reins.

Small cold horse,
how the knife's bloom spills its perfume!

In the dark of the moon
the flanks of the mountain
of Sierra Morena bled.

Where, small sad horse,
are you taking your dead rider?

The night sets spurs
to its black flanks
and pierces with stars.

Small cold horse,
how the knife's bloom spills its perfume!

In the dark of the moon
a scream! And the bonfire's
horn extending.

Where, small sad horse,
are you taking your dead rider?

Afternoon

Three enormous poplars
and a single star.

Silence, nibbled
by frogs, seems
a painted cloth
with moons of green.

In the river
a dried up tree
sheds flowers of
circles in circles.

And I have dreamed
above the waters
of a dark young girl
of Granada.

Rider's Song

Cordoba
afar and alone.

Black pony, huge moon,
green olives in my saddlebag.

Although I know the road,
I'll not reach Cordoba.

Over the plain and through the wind,
my pony black and the moon red,
Death is watching out for me,
from the towers of Cordoba.

O, how long is the road!
O, how brave my pony!
O, for Death that will meet me
before I reach Cordoba!

Cordoba
afar and alone.

Tree, Tree

Tree, Tree,
dry and green.

The girl with the lovely face
is gathering olives.
The wind that courts towers
takes her by the waist.
Four horsemen pass
on Andalusian ponies,
in blue and green suits
and long dark cloaks.
'Come to Cordoba, girl.'
The girl does not listen.
Three slender-waisted
young bullfighters pass
in suits of bright orange
with swords of old silver.
'Come to Seville, girl.'
The girl does not listen.
As evening grows purple
with wide-spreading light,
a youth passes, bearing
moon-roses and myrtle.
'Come to Granada, girl' —
and the girl does not listen;
the girl with the lovely face
goes on picking olives,
the arm of the wind
grey round her waist.

Tree, tree,
dry and green.

The Rising Moon

In the rising moon
the bells are stilled,
and footpaths one cannot follow
come to light.

In the rising moon
the land is covered by sea,
and the heart feels itself an island
in infinity.

No-one eats oranges
in the full of the moon.
The fruit that one must eat
is green and chill.

Under the rising moon
with its hundred similar faces,
coins of silver
are sobbing in the pocket.

Street of the Mutes

Behind the unmoving window panes,
young girls are toying with smiles.

    (In the empty pianos the spiders
    jump round like puppets.)

The young girls talk to their beaux
and swing their tight braids.

    (This is the world of the fan,
    the handkerchief and the hand.)

The beaux respond, making replicas
of blossoms and wings with black capes.

The First Anniversary

This girl walks through my forehead.
It is an age-old feeling.

I ask myself: What's the use
of paper and ink and verse?

To me your body's a crimson
lily, a fresh young reed.

Dark girl in the full of the moon,
what does my desire desire?

23

The Second Anniversary

The moon plunges its huge
horn of light in the sea,

a green and grey unicorn,
tremulous, but in rapture.
The sky floats over the air
like an enormous lotus.

You alone are strolling
the farthest farm of the night.

Flower

The wonderful willow
of the rain downfalling.

O, the rounded moon
above the white boughs.

He Died at Dawn

Four moons in the night
and one lonely tree
with only one shadow
and one lonely bird.

I seek on my body
the print of your lips.
The fountain kissing
the wind without touching.

The *no* that you gave me
I hold in my palm,
a lemon of wax
turned almost white.

Four moons in the night
and one lonely tree.
On the point of a pin
my love spins.

An Unmarried Woman at Mass

Half asleep beneath
the Moses of incense,

the eyes of the bull are watching
your rosary beads rain down.

In your dress of heavy silk
do not move, Virginia.

Give your breasts' black melons
to the droning of the Mass.

Farewell

Should I die, leave open
the door to the balcony.

The urchin is eating an orange.
(I can see him from my balcony.)

The reaper is reaping the wheat.
(I can sense him from my balcony.)

Should I die, leave open
the door to the balcony.

The Mute Boy

The boy hunts for his voice.
(It is held by the king of the crickets.)
In a water drop the boy
is hunting for his voice.

I do not want it for talking.
I will make it into a ring
for my silence to wear
on its little finger.

In a water drop the boy
is hunting for his voice.

Far off, the captured voice
slips on a cricket's robes.

Suicide

The young man forgot himself.
It was ten o'clock in the morning.

His heart was filling with broken
wings and flowers of cloth.

He discovered that nothing remained
in his mouth but a single word.

When he peeled off his gloves, a soft
ash fell from his hands.

He glimpsed a tower from the balcony,
himself both balcony and tower.

Doubtless he saw how in its case
the stopped clock watched him.

He saw his shadow, stretched out and still,
on the white silk divan.

And the young man, stiff, geometrical,
shattered the glass with an axe.

At its breaking, a huge spurt of darkness
flooded his unreal bedroom.

Narcissus

Narcissus.
Your perfume.
And the deep of the stream.

I long to stay on your brink,
love's blossom.
Narcissus.

Shadows and fish, entranced
pass through your white eyes;
butterflies and birds
are laquering mine.

You tiny and I so tall.
Love's blossom.
Narcissus.

The frogs are far too busy
to let stillness touch the mirror
in which your rapture, my rapture,
gaze at one another.

Narcissus.
My sorrow.
And the likeness of my sorrow.

Little Madrigal

Four pomegranates
possess your garden.

(Accept my newborn heart.)

Four cypresses will
possess your garden.

(Accept my ancient heart.)

Sun and moon.
And soon...
no heart!
no garden!

Echo

The flower of the dawn
has already opened.

(Do you recall
the deep of the afternoon?)

The lily of the moon
spills its chill perfume.

(Do you recall
the long gaze of August?)

Desire of a Statue

Hearsay.
Though nothing remains but hearsay.

Perfume.
Though nothing remains but perfume.

Nevertheless rip memory out of me
and the colours of the long gone hours.

Pain.
Coming face to face with live magical pain.

Struggle.
The authentic, the filthy struggle.

Nevertheless, throw out the invisible people
who are moving year on year around my house.

Song of the Barren Orange Tree

Woodchopper,
chop away my shadow.
Let me escape the pain of seeing
myself with no fruit.

Why was I born between mirrors?
Day rings me round,
and night is mimicking me
in all of the stars.

I long to live without seeing
myself. I'll imagine that ants
and flying thistledown
are my leaves, my birds.

Woodchopper,
chop away my shadow.
Let me escape the pain of seeing
myself with no fruit.

II

1924 - 1935

Preciosa and the Wind

Tapping her moon of parchment,
Preciosa comes
down an amphibious path
of laurel bushes and mirrors.
A silence without stars,
running away from the tapping,
falls where the sea beats out
its songs of the fish-filled night.
Upon the heights of the mountain
the soldiers are lying asleep,
guarding the white towers
where the English are living,
and the water-gypsies
are building for their amusement
little arbours of snail shells
and twigs of the green pine.

* * *

Tapping her moon of parchment,
Preciosa comes.
The never-sleeping wind,
on seeing her, rises up.
Saint Christopher, buck-naked,
filled with celestial tongues,
considers the playing girl,
a gentle straying flute.

'Sweet child, let me lift up
your frock so I may see you.
Open for my old fingers
the blue rose of your belly.'

35

Preciosa, dropping
her tambourine, ran without stopping;
the man-in-the-wind pursued her
with his burning sword.

The sea tucks away its rumours.
The olive trees turn white.
The shadowy flutes are singing
and the smooth gong of the snow.

Run, Preciosa, Run!
Or be trapped by the green wind.
Run, Preciosa, run.
Look where he is coming,
a Satyr of fallen stars,
with his glittering tongues.

* * *

Filled with fear, Preciosa
scampers into the mansion
of the English Consul
that is taller than pines.

Startled awake by her cries
three of the soldiers come,
wrapped in their capes of black
their hats firm on their heads.

The Englishman gives the gypsy
a tumbler of warm milk
and a shot of gin
that she does not drink.

As, weeping, she retells
her adventure to these people,
the furious wind is chewing
the tiles of the slate roof.

The Unfaithful Wife

I took her down to the river
believing her a girl
but she had a husband already.
Saint James' night it was,
and almost a kind of duty.
The lamps in the street went out,
and the crickets all lit up.
On the last street corner
I touched her sleeping breasts,
and suddenly they opened
to me like hyacinth spikes.
The stiff starch of her petticoat
made a sound in my ears
like a length of silk
being ripped by ten knives.
With no silver street-light on
their leaves, trees grew immense,
and a horizon of dogs
were barking far from the river.

Past the bramble bushes,
the thorn trees and the reeds,
under the fall of her hair
I scooped a hole in the earth.
I threw away my tie
and she discarded her dress,
then I my belt and revolver
and she her four underskirts.
Neither mother-of-pearl
nor nard could be as smooth

as her skin, nor did silver
or crystal shine as bright.
Her thighs slid away from me
like two astonished fish,
fashioned half of fire,
half made out of ice.
That night I rode along
the finest path of all,
upon a mare of pearl
without stirrup or bridle.
As a man, I cannot repeat
the things she told me then.
The light of understanding
has made me more discreet.
Smeared with kisses and sand,
I led her from the river.
The shining blades of lilies
beat down the air.

I acted as what I am,
a pure-bred gypsy.
I gave her a big satin basket,
straw-coloured for her sewing,
and would not fall in love,
for though she had a husband
she had told me she was a girl
when I took her to the river.

Ballad of the Sleepwalker

Green, green, I want you.
Green breeze. Green boughs.
The ship on the ocean
the horse on the hill.
Waist girdled by shadow,
she dreams at her railing,
skin green, hair green,
eyes of chill silver.
Green, green, I want you.
Under a Romany moon
all things watch her,
but she sees nothing.

Green, green, I want you.
Great frost-stars accompany
the fishes of shadow
opening dawn's highway.
Fig-trees rub the wind
with boughs of sandpaper,
and the mountain, an alley cat,
bristles with bitterness.
Who comes? From where?
At her railing she lingers,
skin green, hair green,
dreams of the sour sea.

'Old friend, I want to swap
my horse for your house,
my saddle for your mirror,
my blade for your blanket.

I come bleeding, old friend,
from the passes of Cabra.'
'Young man, if I could,
I would seal that agreement
but I'm not my own man,
nor my house now mine.'
'Old friend, I want to die
in my bed, decently,
on a bedstead of iron
with fine linen sheets.
Can't you see this great gash
from my chest to my gullet?'
'Three hundred red roses
lie on your white shirt.
Your hot blood is oozing
through your bandage,
but I'm not my own man,
nor is my house mine.'

'At least let me climb
up high to your balcony,
to the balconies of green,
moon-balconies where
there are sounds of water.'

The two friends ascended
to the roof balcony
leaving a bloody spoor,
leaving a spoor of tears.
Little tin lanterns
shook on the rooftops,
dawn pierced by a thousand
tambourine's crystals.

Green, green, I want you.
Green breeze. Green boughs.
The two friends ascended,
the strong wind leaving
a taste in the mouth
of mint, gall, sweet basil.
'Old friend, where is she?
Where is your sad girl?
She was waiting so long,
cheeks cool, hair dark,
in the balcony's green.'

The romany girl
sways over the cistern
skin green, hair green,
eyes of chill silver.
An icicle moon beam
holds her over the water.
The night grew as cosy
as a little town square.
Civil Guards, drunken,
were hammering her door.
Green, green, I want you.
Green breeze. Green boughs.
The ship on the ocean.
The horse on the hill.

Ballad of One Condemned to Death

Solitude, sleepless!
The small eyes of my body,
my horse's enormous ones,
never close through the night,
nor look where a dream
of thirteen boats vanishes.
Instead, clean and strong,
vigilant attendants,
my eyes seek a north
of crags and of metal
where my body with no vein on it
reads packs of ice-white cards.

Huge water oxen charge
lads bathing between the rippling
crescent moons of their horns
and the hammers are chanting
on sleepwalking anvils
insomnias of rider,
insomnias of horse.

On June twenty-fifth
they declared to Amargo:
You may cut, if you wish,
the courtyard's oleander,
daub a cross on your door
and write your name under,
for hemlock and nettle
will root in your side
and needles of wet lime

eat into your shoes.
It will be shadowy night
on the magnetic mountains
where big water oxen,
dreaming, drink in the reeds.
Ask for lamplight and bells,
learn to fold up your hands,
to taste that chill air
of crags and of metal
for inside two months
you will lie in your shroud.

A broadsword of cloud
swings above Santiago.
Deep silence streams
down the sky's curved back.
On June twenty-fifth
Amargo's eyes opened
and now on the twenty-fifth
of August they close.
Men moved down the street
to view the condemned one,
on the wall his dark shadow
of solitude at peace.
And the faultless sheet
with its hard Roman accent
brought balance to death
with its stiff straight folds.

The Taking of Antonito El Camborio on the Road to Seville

Antonio Torres Heredía,
a Camborio son and grandson,
carrying a switch of willow,
is travelling to Seville
to take a look at the bulls,
walking slow and easy,
black-haired as the unripe moon,
with his well-oiled ringlets
glistening above his eyes.
Half way on his journey,
he cut some nice round lemons,
squeezing them, throwing them in
the water till it was gold,
then half way on the journey,
beneath an elm tree's branches
the Civil Guard's highway patrol
took him by both arms.

Slowly the day is passing,
and, hung from one shoulder, the cape
of evening is making a sweep
over the streams and the sea.
The olives are awaiting
the night of Capricorn,
and a quick colt of a breeze
is leaping the leaden mountains.
Antonio Torres Heredía,
Camborio son and grandson,

without his switch of willow,
comes in between five tricorn hats.

Antonio, what are you?
If you are called Camborio,
you should have made a fountain
of blood with five jets.
You are no one's son,
and no real Camborio.
The gypsies are all finished
that strode the mountains alone.
Their knives of old are lying
shuddering in their graves.

This night at nine o'clock
they shut him up in jail,
while the civil guards
are all drinking lemonade.
At nine o'clock at night
while the sky still shines
like the glossy rump of a colt.

The Death of Antonito El Camborio

Death's voices sounded out
beside the Guadalquivir,
old voices gathering round
the virile carnation's voice.
He fastened on their boots
with the bites of a savage boar.
He plunged into the fight
with the slippery leaps of a dolphin.
Bathed in his enemies blood,
his cravat grew crimson,
but he was facing four knives
and could not but succumb.
As the stars were plunging
their lances in grey waters,
and the young bulls dreaming
veronica-swirls of wallflowers,
Death's voices sounded out
beside the Guadalquivir.

'Antonio Torres Heredía,
a stiff-necked Camborio,
dark in the unripe moon
with a virile voice of carnation,
who was it took your life
beside the Guadalquivir?'
'My four Heredía Cousins,
the sons of Benameji,
what they did not envy in others
they found to envy in me,
my shoes the colour of cherries,

my ivory lockets, and
my smoothness of skin in which
olives and jasmine blend.'
'Oh, Antonito el Camborio,
deserving of any Empress,
remember now the Virgin,
for you are about to die.'
'Oh Federico Garcia,
call out the Civil Guard.
They have broken the length of me
in two, like a stalk of corn.'

It took three gushes of blood
to finish it, then he died,
a coin of life that never
would be made again.
A pompous angel places
his head on a cushion.
Four others, flushed and weary,
put light to a candle,
and when his four close cousins
got back to Benameji,
Death's voices ceased to sound
beside the Guadalquivir.

Ballad of the Civil Guard

The horses are black
and black the horseshoes.
Ink stains and wax
glisten on the dark capes.
With their lead-lined skulls
they cannot weep tears.
Their souls patent leather,
they march down the roads,
hump-backed and nocturnal.
Wherever they venture,
a black rubbery hush,
a fine sand of terror.
They go where they wish,
and secrete in their skulls
a restless astronomy
of phantasmal guns.

O Gypsy City,
with flag-bedecked corners,
the moon and the pumpkin,
the bottles of cherries.
O Gypsy City,
seen once, unforgettable,
city of grief and musk,
towers of cinnamon.

At nightfall, the night
made night-black by nightfall,
in smithies, the gypsies
forge arrows and suns.
Sorely wounded, a rider

knocks at all doorways,
and cocks of glass crow
for Jerez of the Frontier.
The naked wind turns
astonishment's corner,
in the silver-black night
made night-black at nightfall.

Saints Joseph and Mary,
their castanets lost,
hunt for the gypsies
to see if they've found them.
The Virgin is dressed
in a Mayoress' robe
of chocolate wrappers,
a necklace of almonds,
and Joseph's arms move
within a silk cloak;
and Pedro Domecque
marches behind them
with three Persian sultans.
The half moon is dreaming,
an ecstatic stork,
as banners and beacons
take over flat roofs.
In the weeping mirrors
are slim-hipped dancers.
Water and shadow, water and shadow
by Jerez of the Frontier.

O Gypsy City,
with flags at the corners,
dowse your green lamps,
the Civil Guard's coming.

O Gypsy City,
once seen, unforgettable.
(Let her stay far from tides
with no combs in her hair.)

Two by two, they advance
on the city fiesta,
immortelles rustling
in bandoliers.
Two by two, they ride in,
twin nocturnes of cloth,
imagining the sky
a glass case of spurs.

The unfearing city
opens more and more doors.
Two score Civil Guards
stormed in to plunder.
All the clocks stopped
and the brandy, in bottles,
looked dead as November
to rouse no suspicion.
Prolonged screams ascended
in flight among weathervanes.
Sabres slashed breezes,
hooves trampled under.
Through the streets shadows,
old gypsies are fleeing
with half asleep horses
and jars filled with coins,
and up the steep streets,
the sinister fleeing
capes, behind them
a cyclone of scissors.

At Bethlehem Gate
the gypsies are gathered.
Saint Joseph, wounded,
shrouds a young girl.
The insistent sharp guns
clatter all the night long
as the Virgin heals infants
with the spittle of stars.
But the Civil Guard comes
and is scattering the bonfires.
Imagination,
young, naked, is seared.
Rose of the Camborios
slumps at her door, moaning,
her two breasts, sliced off,
laid there on a tray,
and other girls flee,
braids flying behind them
in air through which roses
of gunpowder burst.
When every tiled roof
was no more than a furrow,
Dawn simply shrugged
her long profile of stone.

O Gypsy City,
the Civil Guard leaves
through a tunnel of silence,
as flames ring you round.

Gypsy City, once seen,
unforgettable, let them
seek you on my brow.
Play of moon and of sand.

The Martyrdom of Saint Eulalia

1
A Panorama of Merida

A horse with a long tail
is rearing and running
along the street, while
the old Roman soldiers
sleep or play dice. Half
a hill of Minervas
spreads out leafless arms,
and the water, suspended,
gilds edges of stone.
A night of prone torsos
and broken-nosed stars
waits for cracks of the dawn
into which it may topple.
From time to time crimson-
combed blasphemies crow.
The holy girl, groaning,
breaks crystal goblets.
A wheel grinds the knives
and sharp curving hooks.
The anvils' bull bellows,
and Merida is crowned
with half-awake lilies
and briars of bramble.

2
The Martyrdom

Flora walks naked
up the ladders of water.
The Consul commands a tray
for Eulalia's breasts.
A green spurt of veins
breaks out of her throat;
dismayed, her sex trembles,
a bird in a thorn bush.
On the earth, uncontrollably,
her lopped hands, jerking,
still cross in a tenuous
decapitated prayer,
and through the red holes
that once were her breasts,
small skies may be seen
and white streams of milk.
A thousand small trees
of blood clothe her back.
Yellowed centurions,
grey-faced and watchful:
their silver armour's clattering
reaches to the skies.
In the clash of confusion,
the swords' and plumes' fury,
the Consul bears in the
breasts of Eulalia
on a tray, steaming.

3
Hell and Glory

The undulant snow sleeps.
Eulalia, Eulalia
hangs in the branches.
Her charred naked body
blackens the chill air.
The long drawn out night
glistens. Eulalia
is dead in the branches.
The ink in the inkwells
of cities spills slowly.
Tailors' dark dummies
cover snow in the field
with lengthening lines, mourning
their massacred silence.
A scattering of snow
starts falling. Eulalia
is white in the branches,
and nickel squads join
their sharp points in her side.

A peal streaks out
over burned-out skies
between the throats of streams
and of nightingales on the boughs.
Stained glass leaps up!
Eulalia, Eulalia,
white upon white as the
Angels and seraphs cry
Holy, Holy, Holy.

Thamar and Ammon

The moon turns in the sky
over waterless lands,
while the summer sows hiss
of tigers and fire.
Nerves of sheet metal
are ringing on rooftops.
The singed air rises,
bleating from wool.
Earth is delivered up,
wounded and scarred
and shimmering, cauterized
with white lights.

* * *

Thamar was dreaming,
song birds in her throat,
to cool tambourine sounds;
cithars bathed by the moon.
Beneath the eaves, naked,
the pole-star of palms
calls for snows on her belly
and hail on her back.
Thamar on the terrace
was naked and singing,
with five frozen pigeons
encircling her feet.
Ammon on the tower,
sturdy and slender,
stared down upon her,
foam filling his loins,
his bristling beard vibrant.

His radiant nakedness
was stretched out on the terrace,
a chattering between his teeth
like a driven home arrow.
Ammon stared out at
the low and full moon
and saw in the moonlight
his sister's firm breasts.

At half-past three, Ammon
stretched himself out.
His eyes, filled with wings,
made the whole chamber hurt.
The light was so heavy,
it buried whole villages
in brown coloured sand,
and discovered emphemeral
corals of dahlias
and roses. Well-water,
oppressed in its jars,
made silences blossom.
On the moss of the tree trunks
the curled cobra sings,
and Ammon groans in the
cold sheets of his bed.

Shudders, like ivy leaves,
crawl, his hot flesh.
Silently Thamar
came in the still room
blue as veins of the Danube
stirred by the tread
of far off footfalls.

'Thamar, blot out my eyes
with your dawn-bright gaze.
My threads of blood weave
flounces over your lap.'
'Let me be, brother.
The kisses you press
on my shoulder are wasps,
little breezes, deceitful
bee-swarms of flutes.'
'Thamar, in your deep breasts
two fish are calling me,
and your finger palps whisper
of a closely shut rose.'

* * *

The king's hundred horses
neigh in the courtyard.
Slim vines in their tubs
are resisting the sun.
Already he's grabbing her hair
and clawing her clothing.
Tepid corals sketch streams
on a blonde map.

* * *

O what screams were heard
rising over the housetops.
What a thicket of daggers
and ripped apart tunics!
Slaves move up and down
the sadness of stairways.
Thighs and pistons play games
under unmoving clouds.
Gypsy virgins are screaming
round Thamar, and others

are gathering the drops
from her martyred flower.
White clothes turn red
in the shut up rooms.
A tepid dawn, stirring,
transforms leaves and fish.

* * *

Ammon, the wild rapist,
flees on his pony.
Negroes shoot arrows
from the walls and the towers,
and when the four hooves were
no more than four drumbeats,
King David with scissors
cut his harp strings.

Lament for Ignacio Sanchez Mejias

1
Cogida and Death

At five in the afternoon,
on the very point of five,
a lad brought in the white sheet.
It was five in the afternoon.
A basket of lime was ready
that afternoon at five.
The rest was death and only death
at five in the afternoon.

Wind blew away its cotton wool
that afternoon at five.
Dove and leopard struggled together
at five in the afternoon,
and a thigh with a horn of grief.
It was five in the afternoon
when the telling refrain began
at five in the afternoon
green-stained bells and smoke
at five in the afternoon
knots of people in silent corners
at five in the afternoon
and a lone proud-hearted bull
in the afternoon at five
as snowy sweat was coming
at five in the afternoon
and iodine stained the bull-ring
that afternoon at five.

Death laid eggs in the wound
at five in the afternoon,
on the very stroke of five it was,
at five in the afternoon.
His bed was a coffin on wheels
at five in the afternoon.
The music of flutes and bones
filled his ears in the afternoon.
The bull still bellowed in his skull
at five in the afternoon,
the room ablaze with agony
at five in the afternoon.
Lilies were trumpets of green loins
at five in the afternoon,
the red wounds fiery as suns
at five in the afternoon,
and the crowd was breaking in windows
that deadly afternoon
at five; it was five on the clocks
in the shadowed afternoon.

2
The Spilled Blood

I will not look on it.

Command the moon to arrive
for I will not see Ignacio's
blood in the arena.

I will not look.

The free unfettered moon
the motionless horse of cloud

the grey arena of dreams
willows on the barriers.

I won't look.

Let memory burn away.
Inform the jasmines
with their minuscule whiteness.

I will not look.

The old cow of the world
slid a sad tongue
over a bloody muzzle
spilled in the arena,
and the bulls of Guisando,
half stone, half death,
bellowed as if
two hundred years
worn out with pacing
the earth. No.
I will not see it.
I won't look.

Ignacio climbs the steps
with his death on his back.
He was looking for dawn
but the dawn was not there.
He was looking for strength
in his own profile
but a dream confused him.
He was looking
for his handsome body,
and he found blood.

I will not see it.
I will not hear it spurt,
growing feebler each time,
each spurt enlightening
the tiers of benches,
spilling over the thirsty
crowd's corduroy and leather.
Don't ask me to look.

His eyes did not close
when they saw the horns nearing,
but the horrible mothers
lifted their heads
and over the ranches
arose spectral voices
crying aloud to
herdsmen of pale mist.

No Prince of Seville
was ever his equal,
no sword like his sword,
and no heart as true.
His wonderful strength
was a river of lions,
his firm moderation
a torso of marble.
Andalusian Rome
was gold on his head,
his sweet smile a lily
of wisdom and wit.
In the ring a grand fighter,
in the fields a fine peasant,
gentle with wheatsheaves,
decisive with spurs,

superb with the final
bandilleros of darkness.

His sleep has no ending.
Now mosses and grasses,
with sure fingers, probe
and part his skull's petals,
and now his red blood,
as it runs out, is singing,
singing all over the
meadows and marshes.
Sliding on horns of the
frost, in mist shuddering
without a soul, stumbling
on hooves by the thousand,
a long sombre tongue
shaping him a deep pool
of agony close to the
starry Guadalquivir.
O white wall of Spain.
O black bull of mourning,
O strong blood of Ignacio,
his veins' nightingale.
No.

I won't look.

No cup can contain it,
no swallow sip it,
no bright frost, no song,
no deep deluge chill it,
and no mirror cover it
over with silver.
No.
I won't look.

The Corpse Laid Out

Stone is a brow of sorrowing dreams
with no swerve of water or frozen cypress.
Stone is a shoulder that carries Time
with trees of tears and ribbons and stars.

I have watched grey rains greyly race on the waves,
lifting their delicate speckled arms
to escape from the trap of the stone's lie
that loosens their members without shedding blood.

For stone brings the clouds and the seed together,
the skeletal larks and crepuscular wolves,
but offers no sounds, no crystals, no flames,
only bull-rings and bull-rings and more without walls.

Now high-born Ignacio lies on the stone,
everything ended. What will now happen?
Look on his face. Death swathes him in sulphur
and gives him the head of a dark minotaur.

Everything's ended. The rain fills his mouth.
The air, as if crazed, leaves his caved-in chest,
and love, drenched and soaked with tears of the snow,
is warming itself on the horns of the herd.

What are they saying? Stinking silence is settling.
We are here with a laid-out body that fades,
with a pure form that nightingales had for a dwelling,
and we watch as it fills with fathomless holes.

Who crumples the shroud? It's not true what they say.
No one sings here or cries in the corner.
Nobody jabs spurs or frightens the serpent.
I need nothing more than my wide-open eyes
to look on this body that cannot find peace.

I want to see here those hard voiced men,
the breakers of horses and tamers of rivers,
those strongly framed men that know how to sing
with mouths that are filled with sun and with flint.

I must see them here in front of that stone,
their horses' reins broken in front of this body.
From them I must learn the way to escape
for the sake of this captain fettered by death.

I want them to bring me laments that like rivers
have delicate mists and deep curving banks,
to carry Ignacio's body to where
it may lose itself far from the snorts of the bulls,

where it may lose itself in the moon's round bullring
that pretends in its youth a quiet sad bull,
where it may lose itself in a night without fish songs
and in the white thicket of frozen smoke.

I don't want them to cover his carrying death.
Ignacio, Go! Do not feel the hot bellowings.
Sleep! Fly! Find rest! Even oceans die.

4

The Absent Spirit

Neither the bull nor the fig tree know you,
nor the ants nor the horses in your house.
The child and the afternoon do not know you,
because now you are dead for ever.

Even the back of the stone does not know you,
nor the black satin in which you rot.
Your silent memories do not know you,
because now you are dead for ever.

Because now you are dead for ever
like all the dead of the whole earth,
like all the dead who are long forgotten
in a huge heap of lifeless dogs.

Nobody knows you, but I sing of you.
For the future I sing of your grace and figure,
of your understanding's mature strength,
of your hunger for death and the touch of its mouth,
of the sadness of your brave gaiety gone.

It will be long years, if ever, before
another Andalusian's born
so full of truth, so hot with adventure.
I sing of his grace with words that groan,
and recall a sad breeze through the olive trees.

• Cap-Saint-Ignace
• Sainte-Marie (Beauce)
Québec, Canada
1997